Apostolic Letter

THE LIGHT
OF THE EAST

Orientale Lumen

Apostolic Letter

THE LIGHT OF THE EAST

Orientale Lumen

of the Supreme Pontiff
John Paul II

To the Bishops, Clergy and Faithful
to Mark the Centenary
of *Orientale Dignitas*
of Pope Leo XIII

BOOKS & MEDIA

BOSTON

Vatican Translation

ISBN 0-8198-4478-0

Copyright © 1995, Daughters of St. Paul

Printed and published in the U.S.A. by Pauline Books & Media, 50 St. Paul's Avenue, Boston, MA 02130.

www.pauline.org   e-mail: pbm edit@interramp.com

Pauline Books & Media is the publishing house of the Daughters of St. Paul, an international congregation of women religious serving the Church with the communications media.

CONTENTS

I. Knowing the Christian East An Experience of Faith 17

Gospel, Churches and Culture 21
   Between memory and expectation 22
   Monasticism as a model of baptismal life 25

Between Word and Eucharist 27
   *A liturgy for the whole man and
   for the whole cosmos* 29
   A clear look at self-discovery 31
   A father in the Spirit 32
   Communion and service 34
   A person in relationship 35
   An adoring silence 37

II. From Knowledge to Encounter 39

Experiences of unity 44
*Meeting one another, getting to know one another,
working together* 48
Journeying together toward the "Orientale Lumen" 54

Venerable Brothers,
Dear Sons and Daughters of the Church

1. The light of the East has illumined the universal Church, from the moment when "a rising sun" appeared above us *(Lk* 1:78): Jesus Christ, our Lord, whom all Christians invoke as the Redeemer of man and the hope of the world.

That light inspired my predecessor Pope Leo XIII to write the Apostolic Letter *Orientalium Dignitas* in which he sought to safeguard the significance of the Eastern traditions for the whole Church.[1]

On the centenary of that event and of the initiatives the Pontiff intended at that time as an aid to restoring unity with all the Christians of the East, I wish to send to the Catholic Church a similar appeal, which has been enriched by the knowledge and interchange which has taken place over the past century.

Since, in fact, we believe that the venerable and ancient tradition of the Eastern Churches is an integral part of the heritage of Christ's Church, the first need for Catholics is *to be*

---

1. Cf. *Leonis XIII Acta,* 14 (1894), 358 370. The Pope recalls the esteem and the concrete help which the Holy See has given the Eastern Churches, and its willingness to safeguard their specific qualities; in addition, cf. Apostolic Letter *Praeclara gratulationis* (June 20, 1894), *l.c.,* 195 214, Encyclical Letter *Christi Nomen* (December 24, 1894), *l.c.,* 405-409.

familiar with that tradition, so as to be nourished by it and to encourage the process of unity in the best way possible for each.

Our Eastern Catholic brothers and sisters are very conscious of being the living bearers of this tradition, together with our Orthodox brothers and sisters. The members of the Catholic Church of the Latin tradition must also be fully acquainted with this treasure and thus feel, with the Pope, a passionate longing that *the full manifestation of the Church's catholicity* be restored to the Church and to the world, expressed not by a single tradition, and still less by one community in opposition to the other; and that we too may be granted a full taste of the divinely revealed and undivided heritage of the universal Church[2] which is preserved and grows in the life of the Churches of the East as in those of the West.

2. My gaze turns to the *Orientale Lumen* which shines from Jerusalem (cf. *Is* 60:1; *Rev* 21:10), the city where the Word of God, made man for our salvation, a Jew "descended from David according to the flesh" *(Rom* 1:3; *2 Tim* 2:8), died and rose again. In that holy city, when the day of Pentecost had come and "they were all together in one place *(Acts* 2:1), the Paraclete was sent upon Mary and the disciples. From there the Good News spread throughout the world because, filled with the Holy Spirit, "they spoke the word of God with boldness" *(Acts* 4:31). From there, from the mother of all the Churches,[3]

---

2. Cf. Second Vatican Ecumenical Council, Decree on the Eastern Catholic Churches *Orientialium Ecclesiarum,* 1; Decree on Ecumenism *Unitatis Redintegratio,* 17.

3. Saint Augustine notes in this regard: "From where did the Church spread? From Jerusalem," *In Epistulam Ioannis,* II, 2: PL 35, 1990.

the Gospel was preached to all nations, many of which boast of having had one of the Apostles as their first witness to the Lord.[4] In that city the most varied cultures and traditions were welcomed in the name of the one God (cf. *Acts* 2:9-11). In turning to it with nostalgia and gratitude, we find the strength and enthusiasm to intensify *the quest for harmony* in that genuine plurality of forms which remains the Church's ideal.[5]

3. A Pope, son of a Slav people, is particularly moved by the call of those peoples to whom the two saintly brothers Cyril and Methodius went. They were a glorious example of apostles of unity who were able to proclaim Christ in their search for communion between East and West amid the difficulties which sometimes set the two worlds against one another. Several times I have reflected on the example of their activity,[6] also addressing those who are their children in faith and culture.

These considerations now need to be broadened so as to embrace all the Eastern Churches, in the variety of their different traditions. My thoughts turn to our brothers and sisters of the Eastern Churches, in the wish that together we may seek the strength of an answer to the questions man is asking today in every part of the world. I intend to address their heritage of faith and life, aware that there can be no second thoughts about pursuing the path of unity, which is irreversible as the Lord's appeal for unity is irreversible. "Dearly beloved, we have this

---

4. Cf. Second Vatican Ecumenical Council, Dogmatic Constitution on the Church *Lumen Gentium,* 23; Decree on Ecumenism *Unitatis Redintegratio,* 14.

5. Cf. Second Vatican Ecumenical Council, Decree on Ecumenism *Unitatis Redintegratio,* 4.

6. Cf. Apostolic Letter *Egregiae Virtutis* (December 31, 1980): *AAS* 73 (1981), 258-262; Encyclical Letter *Slavorum Apostoli* (June 2, 1985), 12-14: *AAS* 77, (1985), 792-796

common task: we must say together from East and West: *Ne evacuetur Crux!* (cf. *1 Cor* 1:17). The cross of Christ must not be emptied of its power because if the cross of Christ is emptied of its power, man no longer has roots, he no longer has prospects: he is destroyed! This is the cry of the end of the 20th century. It is the cry of Rome, of Moscow, of Constantinople. It is the cry of all Christendom: of the Americas, of Africa, of Asia, of everyone. It is the cry of the new evangelization."[7]

I am thinking of the Eastern Churches, as did many other Popes in the past, aware that the mandate to preserve the Church's unity and to seek Christian unity tirelessly wherever it was wounded was addressed to them. A particularly close link already binds us. We have almost everything in common;[8] and above all, we have in common the true longing for unity.

4. The cry of men and women today seeking meaning for their lives reaches all the Churches of the East and of the West. In this cry, we perceive the invocation of those who seek the Father whom they have forgotten and lost (cf. *Lk* 15:18-20; *Jn* 14:8). The women and men of today are asking us to show them Christ, who knows the Father and who has revealed him (cf. *Jn* 8:55; 14:8-11). Letting the world ask us its questions, listening with humility and tenderness, in full solidarity with those who express them, *we are called to show in word an deed today the immense riches that our Churches preserve in the coffers of their traditions.* We learn from the Lord himself, who would stop along the way to be with the people, who listened to

---

7. Address after the Way of the Cross, Good Friday (April 1, 1994), 3: *AAS* 87, (1995), 88.

8. Cf. Second Vatican Ecumenical Council, Decree on Ecumenism *Unitatis Redintegratio,* 14-18.

them and was moved to pity when he saw them "like sheep without a shepherd" *(Mt* 9:36; cf. *Mk* 6:34). From him we must learn the loving gaze with which he reconciled men with the Father and with themselves, communicating to them that power which alone is able to heal the whole person.

This appeal calls on the Churches of the East and the West to concentrate on the essential: "We cannot come before Christ, the Lord of history, as divided as we have unfortunately been in the course of the second millennium. These divisions must give way to *rapprochement* and harmony; the wounds on the path of Christian unity must be healed."[9]

Going beyond our own frailties, we must turn to him, the one Teacher, sharing in his death so as to purify ourselves from that jealous attachment to feelings and memories, not of the great things God has done for us, but of the human affairs of a past that still weighs heavily on our hearts. May the Spirit clarify our gaze so that together we may reach out to contemporary man who is waiting for the good news. If we make a *harmonious,* illuminating, life-giving *response* to the world's expectations and sufferings, we will truly contribute to a more effective proclamation of the Gospel among the people of our time.

---

9. Address to the Extraordinary Consistory (June 13, 1994): *L'Osservatore Romano,* June 13-14, 1994), p. 5

I

KNOWING THE CHRISTIAN EAST AN EXPERIENCE OF FAITH

5. "In the study of revealed truth East and West have used different methods and approaches in understanding and confessing divine things. It is hardly surprising, then, if sometimes one tradition has come nearer to a full appreciation of some aspects of a mystery of revelation than the other, or has expressed them better. In such cases, these various theological formulations are often to be considered complementary rather than conflicting."[10]

Pondering over the questions, aspirations and experiences I have mentioned, my thoughts turn to the Christian heritage of the East. I do not intend to describe that heritage or to interpret it: I listen to the Churches of the East, which I know are living interpreters of the treasure of tradition they preserve. In contemplating it, before my eyes appear elements of great significance for fuller and more thorough understanding of the Christian experience. These elements are capable of giving a more complete Christian response to the expectations of the men and women of today. Indeed, in comparison to any other culture, the Christian East has a unique and privileged role as the original setting where the Church was born. The Christian tradition of the East implies a way of accepting, understanding

---

10. Second Vatican Ecumenical Council, Decree on Ecumenism *Unitatis Redintegratio,* 17.

and living faith in the Lord Jesus. In this sense it is extremely close to the Christian tradition of the West, which is born of and nourished by the same faith. Yet it is legitimately and admirably distinguished from the latter, since Eastern Christians have their own way of perceiving and understanding, and thus an original way of living their relationship with the Savior. Here, with respect and trepidation, I want to approach the act of worship which these Churches express, rather than to identify this or that specific theological point which has emerged down the centuries in the polemical debates between East and West.

From the beginning, the Christian East has proved to contain a wealth of forms capable of assuming the characteristic features of each individual culture, with supreme respect for each particular community. We can only thank God with deep emotion for the wonderful variety with which he has allowed such a rich and composite mosaic of different tesserae to be formed.

6. Certain features of the spiritual and theological tradition, common to the various Churches of the East mark their sensitivity to the forms taken by the transmission of the Gospel in Western lands. The Second Vatican Council summarized them as follows: "Everyone knows with what love the Eastern Christians celebrate the sacred liturgy, especially the Eucharistic mystery, source of the Church's life and pledge of future glory. In this mystery the faithful, united with their bishops, have access to God the Father through the Son, the Word made flesh who suffered and was glorified, in the outpouring of the Holy Spirit. And so, made 'sharers of the divine nature' *(2 Pt* 1:4) they enter into communion with the Most Holy Trinity."[11]

---

11. Second Vatican Ecumenical Council, Decree on Ecumenism *Unitatis Redintegratio,* 15.

These features describe the Eastern outlook of the Christian. His or her goal is participation in the divine nature through communion with the mystery of the Holy Trinity. In this view the Father's "monarchy" is outlined as well as the concept of salvation according to the divine plan, as it is presented by Eastern theology after Saint Irenaeus of Lyons and which spread among the Cappadocian Fathers.[12]

Participation in Trinitarian life takes place through the liturgy and in a special way through the Eucharist, the mystery of communion with the glorified body of Christ, the seed of immortality.[13] In divinization and particularly in the sacraments, Eastern theology attributes a very special role to the Holy Spirit: through the power of the Spirit who dwells in man deification already begins on earth; the creature is transfigured and God's kingdom inaugurated.

The teaching of the Cappadocian Fathers on divinization passed into the tradition of all the Eastern Churches and is part of their common heritage. This can be summarized in the thought already expressed by Saint Irenaeus at the end of the second century: *God passed into man so that man might pass over to God.*[14] This theology of divinization remains one of the achievements particularly dear to Eastern Christian thought.[15]

---

12. Cf. Saint Irenaeus, *Against Heresies* V, 36, 2: *SCh* 153/2, 461; Saint Basil, *Treatise on the Holy Spirit,* XV, 36: *PG* 32, 132; XVII, 43, *l.c.,* 148; XVIII, 47, *l.c.,* 153.

13. Cf. Saint Gregory of Nyssa, *Catechetical Discourse,* XXXVII: *PG* 45, 97.

14. Cf. *Against Heresies* III, 10, 2: *SCh* 211/2, 121; III, 18, 7, *l.c.,* 365; III, 19, 1, *l.c.,* 375; IV, 20, 4: *SCh* 100/2, 635; IV, 33, 4, *l.c.,* 811; V, Pref., *SCh* 153/2, 15.

15. Grafted on Christ, "men become gods and children of God...the dust is raised to such a degree of glory that it is now equal in honor and godliness to the divine nature" Nicholas Cabasilas, *Life in Christ,* I: *PG* 150, 505.

On this path of divinization, those who have been made "most Christ-like" by grace and by commitment to the way of goodness go before us: the martyrs and the saints.[16] And the Virgin Mary occupies an altogether special place among them. From her the shoot of Jesse sprang (cf. *Is* 11:1). Her figure is not only the Mother who waits for us, but the Most Pure, who—the fulfillment of so many Old Testament pre-figurations—is an icon of the Church, the symbol and anticipation of humanity transfigured by grace, the model and the unfailing hope for all those who direct their steps toward the heavenly Jerusalem.[17]

Although strongly emphasizing Trinitarian realism and its unfolding in sacramental life, the East associates faith in the unity of the divine nature with the fact that the divine essence is unknowable. The Eastern Fathers always assert that it is impossible to know what God is; one can only know that he is, since he revealed himself in the history of salvation as Father, Son and Holy Spirit.[18]

This sense of the inexpressible divine reality is reflected in liturgical celebration, where the sense of mystery is so strongly felt by all the faithful of the Christian East.

"Moreover, in the East are to be found the riches of those spiritual traditions which are given expression in monastic life especially. From the glorious times of the holy Fathers that

---

16. Cf. Saint John Damascene, *On Images,* I, 19: *PG* 94, 1249.

17. Cf. John Paul II, Encyclical Letter *Redemptoris Mater,* (March 25, 1987), 31-34 AAS 79 (1987), 402-406; Second Vatican Ecumenical Council, Decree on Ecumenism *Unitatis Redintegratio,* 15.

18. Cf. Saint Irenaeus, *Against Heresies,* II, 28, 3-6: SCh 294, 274-284; Saint Gregory of Nyssa, *Life of Moses*: *PG* 44, 377; Saint Gregory of Nazianzus, *On Holy Easter,* or. XLV, 3ff.; *PG* 36, 625-630.

monastic spirituality flourished in the East which later flowed over into the Western world, and there provided a source from which Latin monastic life took its rise and has often drawn fresh vigor ever since. Therefore, it is earnestly recommended that Catholics avail themselves more often of the spiritual riches of the Eastern Fathers which lift up the whole man to the contemplation of the divine mysteries."[19]

Gospel, Churches and Culture

7. As I have pointed out at other times, one of the first great values embodied particularly in the Christian East is the attention given to peoples and their cultures, *so that the Word of God and his praise my resound in every language.* I reflected on this topic in the Encyclical Letter *Slavorum Apostoli*, where I noted that Cyril and Methodius "desired to become similar in every aspect to those to whom they were bringing the Gospel; they wished to become a part of those peoples and to share their lot in everything";[20] "it was a question of a new method of catechesis."[21]

In doing this, they expressed an attitude widespread in the Christian East: "By incarnating the Gospel in the native culture of the peoples which they were evangelizing, Saints Cyril and Methodius were especially meritorious for the formation and development of that same culture, or rather of many cultures."[22]

---

19. Second Vatican Ecumenical Council, Decree on Ecumenism *Unitatis Redintegratio*, 15.

20. No. 9: *AAS* 77 (1985), 789-790

21. *Ibid.*, 11, *l.c.*, 791

22. *Ibid.*, 21, *l.c.*, 802-803

They combined respect and consideration for individual cultures with a passion for the universality of the Church, which they tirelessly strove to achieve. The attitude of the two brothers from Thessalonica is representative in Christian antiquity of a style typical of many churches: revelation is proclaimed satisfactorily and becomes fully understandable *when Christ speaks the tongues of the various peoples,* and they can read scripture and sing the liturgy in their own language with their own expressions, as though repeating the marvels of Pentecost.

At a time when it is increasingly recognized that the right of every people to express themselves according to their own heritage of culture and thought is fundamental, the experience of the individual Churches of the East is offered to us as an authoritative example of successful inculturation.

From this model we learn that if we wish to avoid the recurrence of particularism as well as of exaggerated nationalism, we must realize that the proclamation of the Gospel should be deeply *rooted in what is distinctive to each culture and open to convergence in a universality,* which involves an exchange for the sake of mutual enrichment.

Between memory and expectation

8. Today we often feel ourselves prisoners of the present. It is as though man had lost his perception of belonging to a history which precedes and follows him. This effort to situate oneself between the past and the future, with a grateful heart for the benefits received and for those expected, is offered by the Eastern Churches in particular, with a clear-cut sense of continuity which takes the name of Tradition and of eschatological expectation.

Tradition is the heritage of Christ's Church. This is a living memory of the Risen One met and witnessed to by the Apostles who passed on his living memory to their successors in an uninterrupted line, guaranteed by the apostolic succession through the laying on of hands, down to the bishops of today. This is articulated in the historical and cultural patrimony of each Church, shaped by the witness of the martyrs, fathers and saints, as well as by the living faith of all Christians down the centuries to our own day. It is not an unchanging repetition of formulas, but a heritage which preserves its original, living kerygmatic core. It is Tradition that preserves the Church from the danger of gathering only changing opinions, and guarantees her certitude and continuity.

When the uses and customs belonging to each Church are considered as absolutely unchangeable, there is a sure risk of Tradition losing that feature of a living reality which grows and develops, and which the Spirit guarantees precisely because it has something to say to the people of every age. As Scripture is increasingly understood by those who read it,[23] every other element of the Church's living heritage is increasingly understood by believers and is enriched by new contributions, *in fidelity and in continuity.*[24] Only a religious assimilation, in the obedience of faith, of what the Church calls "Tradition" will enable Tradition to be embodied in different cultural and historical situations and conditions.[25] Tradition is never pure

---

23. *"Divina eloquia cum legente crescunt"*: Saint Gregory the Great *In Ezekiel*, I, VII, 8: *PL* 76, 843

24. Cf. Second Vatican Ecumenical Council, Dogmatic Constitution on Divine Revelation *Dei Verbum*, 8.

25. Cf. International Theological Commission, *Interpretationis Problema* (October 1989), II, 1-2: *Enchiridion Vaticanum* 11, pp. 1717-1719.

nostalgia for things or forms past, nor regret for lost privileges, but the living memory of the Bride, kept eternally youthful by the Love that dwells within her.

If Tradition puts us in continuity with the past, eschatological expectation opens us to God's future. Each Church must struggle against the temptation to make an absolute of what it does, and thus to celebrate itself or abandon itself to sorrow. But time belongs to God, and whatever takes place in time can never be identified with the fullness of the Kingdom, which is always a free gift. The Lord Jesus came to die for us and rose from the dead, while creation, saved through hope, is still suffering its birth pangs (cf. *Rom* 8:22). The Lord himself will return to give the cosmos to the Father (cf. *1 Cor* 15:28). The Church invokes this return, and the monk and the religious are its privileged witnesses.

The East expresses in a living way the reality of tradition and expectation. All its liturgy, in particular, is a commemoration of salvation and an invocation of the Lord's return. And if Tradition teaches the Churches fidelity to what gave birth to them, *eschatological expectation urges them to be what they have not yet fully become,* what the Lord wants them to become, and thus to seek ever new ways of fidelity, overcoming pessimism because they are striving for the hope of God who does not disappoint.

We must show people the beauty of memory, the power that comes to us from the Spirit and makes us witnesses because *we are children of witnesses;* we must make them taste the wonderful things the Spirit has wrought in history; we must show that it is precisely Tradition which has preserved them, thus giving hope to those who, even without seeing their efforts to do good crowned by success, know that someone else will bring them to fulfillment; therefore man will feel less alone, less enclosed in the narrow corner of his own individual achievement.

Monasticism as a model of baptismal life

9. I would now like to look at the vast panorama of Eastern Christianity from a specific vantage point which affords a view of many of its features: *monasticism.*

In the East, monasticism has retained great unity. It did not experience the development of different kinds of apostolic life as in the West. The various expressions of monastic life, from the strictly cenobitic, as conceived by Pachomius or Basil, to the rigorously eremitic, as with Anthony or Macarius of Egypt, correspond more to different stages of the spiritual journey than to the choice between different states of life. In any event, whatever form they take, they are all based on monasticism.

Moreover, in the East, monasticism was not seen merely as a separate condition, proper to a precise category of Christians, but rather as a reference point for all the baptized, according to the gifts offered to each by the Lord; it was presented as a symbolic synthesis of Christianity.

When God's call is total, as it is in the monastic life, then the person can reach the highest point that sensitivity, culture and spirituality are able to express. This is even more true for the Eastern Churches, for which monasticism was an essential experience and still today is seen to flourish in them, once persecution is over and hearts can be freely raised to heaven. The monastery is the prophetic place where creation becomes praise of God and the precept of concretely lived charity becomes the ideal of human coexistence; it is where the human being seeks God without limitation or impediment, becoming a reference point for all people, bearing them in his heart and helping them to seek God.

I would also like to mention the splendid witness of nuns in the Christian East. This witness has offered an example of giving full value in the Church to what is specifically feminine, even breaking through the mentality of the time. During recent persecutions, especially in Eastern European countries, when many male monasteries were forcibly closed, female monasticism kept the torch of the monastic life burning. The nun's charism, with its own specific characteristics, is a visible sign of that motherhood of God to which Sacred Scripture often refers.

Therefore I will look to monasticism in order to identify those values which I feel are very important today for expressing the contribution of the Christian East to the journey of Christ's Church toward the Kingdom. While these aspects are at times neither exclusive to monasticism nor to the Eastern heritage, they have frequently acquired a particular connotation in themselves. Besides, we are not seeking to make the most of exclusivity, but of the mutual enrichment in what the one Spirit has inspired in the one Church of Christ.

Monasticism has always been the very soul of the Eastern Churches: the first Christian monks were born in the East and the monastic life was an integral part of the Eastern *lumen* passed on to the West by the great Fathers of the undivided Church.[26]

---

26. The *Life of Anthony* written by Saint Athanasius had a great influence in the West: *PG* 26, 835-977. Among others, Saint Augustine refers to it in his *Confessions*, VIII, 6: *CSEL* 33, 181-182. The translations of works by the Eastern Fathers, including the *Rules* of St. Basil: *PG* 31, 889-1305. The *History of the Monks of Egypt*: *PG* 441-456, and the *Apophthegmata of the Desert Fathers*: *PG* 65, 72-440 marked Western monasticism. Cf. Guillaume De Saint Thierry *Epistula ad Fratres de Monte Dei*: *SCh* 223, 130-384.

The strong common traits uniting the monastic experience of the East and the West make it a wonderful bridge of fellowship, where unity as it is lived shines even more brightly than may appear in the dialogue between the Churches.

Between Word and Eucharist

10. Monasticism shows in a special way that life is suspended between two poles: the Word of God and the Eucharist. This means that even in its eremitical forms, it is always a personal response to an individual call and, at the same time, an ecclesial and community event.

The starting point for the monk is the Word of God, a Word who calls, who invites, who personally summons, as happened to the Apostles. When a person is touched by the Word obedience is born, that is, the listening which changes life. Every day the monk is nourished by the bread of the Word. Deprived of it, he is as though dead and has nothing left to communicate to his brothers and sisters because the Word is Christ, to whom the monk is called to be conformed.

Even while he chants with his brothers the prayer that sanctifies time, he continues his assimilation of the Word. The very rich liturgical hymnody, of which all the Churches of the Christian East can be justly proud, is but the continuation of the Word which is read, understood, assimilated and finally sung: those hymns are largely sublime paraphrases of the biblical text, filtered and personalized through the individual's experience and that of the community.

Standing before the abyss of divine mercy, the monk can only proclaim the awareness of his own radical poverty, which immediately becomes a plea for help and a cry of rejoicing on account of an even more generous salvation, since from the abyss of his own wretchedness such salvation is unthinkable.[27] This is why the plea for forgiveness and the glorification of God form a substantial part of liturgical prayer. The Christian is immersed in wonder at this paradox, the latest of an infinite series, all magnified with gratitude in the language of the liturgy: the Immense accepts limitation; a virgin gives birth; through death, he who is life conquers death forever; in the heights of heaven, a human body is seated at the right hand of the Father.

The Eucharist is the culmination of this prayer experience, the other pole indissolubly bound to the Word, as the place where the Word becomes Flesh and Blood, a heavenly experience where this becomes an event.

In the Eucharist, the Church's inner nature is revealed, a community of those summoned to the synaxis to celebrate the gift of the One who is offering and offered: participating in the Holy Mysteries, they become "kinsmen"[28] of Christ, anticipating the experience of divinization in the now inseparable bond linking divinity and humanity in Christ.

But *the Eucharist is also what anticipates the relationship of men and things to the heavenly Jerusalem.* In this way it reveals its eschatological nature completely: as a living sign of this expectation, the monk continues and brings to fulfillment

---

27. Cf. for example, Saint Basil, *Short Rule*: *PG* 31, 1079-1305; Saint John Chrysostom, *On Compunction*: *PG* 47, 391-422; *Homilies on Matthew*, hom. XV, 3: *PG* 57, 225-228; Saint Gregory of Nyssa, *On the Beatitudes*, hom. 3: *PG* 44, 1219-1232.

28. Cf. Nicholas Cabasilas, *Life in Christ*, IV: *PG* 150, 584-585; Cyril of Alexandria, *Treatise on John*, 11: *PG* 74, 561; *ibid.*, 12, *l.c.*, 564; Saint John Chrysostom, *Homilies on Matthew*, Homily LXXXII, 5: *PG* 58, 743-744.

in the liturgy the invocation of the Church, the Bride who implores the Bridegroom's return in a *maranatha* constantly repeated, not only in words, but with the whole of his life.

A liturgy for the whole man and for the whole cosmos

11. In the liturgical experience, Christ the Lord is the light which illumines the way and reveals the transparency of the cosmos, precisely as in Scripture. The events of the past find in Christ their meaning and fullness, and creation is revealed for what it is: a complex whole which finds its perfection, its purpose *in the liturgy* alone. This is why the liturgy is heaven on earth, and in it the Word who became flesh imbues matter with a saving potential which is fully manifest in the sacraments: there, creation communicates to each individual the power conferred on it by Christ. Thus the Lord, immersed in the Jordan, transmits to the waters a power which enables them to become the bath of baptismal rebirth.[29]

Within this framework, liturgical prayer in the East shows a great aptitude for involving the human person in his or her totality: the mystery is sung in the loftiness of its content, but also in the warmth of the sentiments it awakens in the heart of redeemed humanity. In the sacred act, even bodiliness is summoned to praise, and beauty, which in the East is one of the best loved names expressing the divine harmony and the model of humanity transfigured,[30] appears everywhere: in the shape of the church, in the sounds, in the colors, in the lights, in the scents. The lengthy duration of the celebrations, the repeated

---

29. Cf. Saint Gregory of Nazianzus, *Discourse* XXXIX: *PG* 36, 335-360.
30. Cf. Clement of Alexandria, *The Pedagogue,* III, 1, 1: *SCh* 158, 12.

invocations, everything expresses gradual identification with the mystery celebrated with one's whole person. Thus the prayer of the Church already becomes participation in the heavenly liturgy, an anticipation of the final beatitude.

This total involvement of the person in his rational and emotional aspects, in "ecstasy" and in immanence, is of great interest and a wonderful way to understand the meaning of created realities: these are neither an absolute nor a den of sin and iniquity. *In the liturgy, things reveal their own nature as a gift* offered by the Creator to humanity: "God saw everything that he had made, and behold, it was very good" *(Gen* 1:31). Though all this is marked by the tragedy of sin, which weighs down matter and obscures its clarity, the latter is redeemed in the Incarnation and becomes fully "theophoric," that is, capable of putting us in touch with the Father. This property is most apparent in the holy mysteries, the sacraments of the Church.

Christianity does not reject matter. Rather, bodiliness is considered in all its value in the liturgical act, whereby the human body is disclosed in its inner nature as a temple of the Spirit and is united with the Lord Jesus, who himself took a body for the world's salvation. This does not mean, however, an absolute exaltation of all that is physical, for we know well the chaos which sin introduced into the harmony of the human being. The liturgy reveals that the body, through the mystery of the Cross, is in the process of transfiguration, pneumatization: on Mount Tabor Christ showed his body radiant, as the Father wants it to be again.

Cosmic reality also is summoned to give thanks because the whole universe is called to recapitulation in Christ the Lord. This concept expresses a balanced and marvelous teaching on the dignity, respect and purpose of creation and of the human body in particular. With the rejection of all dualism and every cult of pleasure as an end in itself, the body becomes a place made luminous by grace and thus fully human.

To those who seek a truly meaningful relationship with themselves and with the cosmos, so often disfigured by selfishness and greed, the liturgy reveals the way to the harmony of the new man, and invites him to respect the Eucharistic potential of the created world. That world is destined to be assumed in the Eucharist of the Lord, in his Passover, present in the sacrifice of the altar.

A clear look at self-discovery

12. The monk turns his gaze to Christ, God and man. In the disfigured face of Christ, the man of sorrow, he sees the prophetic announcement of the *transfigured* face of the Risen Christ. To the contemplative eye, Christ reveals himself as he did to the women of Jerusalem, who had gone up to contemplate the mysterious spectacle on Calvary. Trained in this school, the monk becomes accustomed to contemplating Christ in the hidden recesses of creation and in the history of mankind, which is then understood from the standpoint of identification with the whole Christ.

This gaze progressively *conformed to Christ* thus learns detachment from externals, from the tumult of the senses, from all that keeps man from that freedom which allows him to be grasped by the Spirit. Walking this path, he is reconciled with Christ in a constant process of conversion: in the awareness of his own sin and of his distance from the Lord which becomes heartfelt remorse, a symbol of his own baptism in the salutary water of tears; in silence and inner quiet, which is sought and given, where he learns to make his heart beat in harmony with the rhythm of the Spirit, eliminating all duplicity and ambiguity. This process of becoming ever more moderate and sparing, more transparent to himself, can cause him to fall into pride and intransigence if he comes to believe that these are the fruits of his own ascetic efforts. Spiritual discernment in continuous purification then makes him humble and meek, aware that he can perceive only some aspects of that truth which fills him, because it is the gift of the Spouse, who alone is fulfillment and happiness.

To the person who is seeking the meaning of life, the East offers this school which teaches one to know oneself and to be free and loved by that Jesus who says: "Come to me, all who labor and are heavy laden, and I will give you rest" *(Mt* 11:28). He tells those who seek inner healing to go on searching: if their intention is upright and their way is honest, in the end the Father's face will let itself be recognized, engraved as it is in the depths of the human heart.

A father in the Spirit

13. A monk's way is not generally marked by personal effort alone. He turns to a spiritual father to whom he abandons himself with filial trust, in the certainty that God's tender and demanding fatherhood is manifested in him. This figure gives Eastern monasticism an extraordinary flexibility: through the spiritual father's intervention the way of each monk is in fact strongly personalized in the times, rhythms and ways of seeking God. Precisely because the spiritual father is the harmonizing link, monasticism is permitted the greatest variety of ceno-

bitic and eremitical expressions. Monasticism in the East has thus been able to fulfill the expectations of each church in the various periods of its history.[31]

In this quest, the East in particular teaches that there are brothers and sisters to whom the Spirit has granted the gift of spiritual guidance. They are precious points of reference, for they see things with the loving gaze with which God looks at us. It is not a question of renouncing one's own freedom, in order to be looked after by others. It is benefiting from the knowledge of the heart, which is a true charism, in order to be helped, gently and firmly, to find the way of truth. Our world desperately needs such spiritual guides. It has frequently rejected them, for they seemed to lack credibility or their example appeared out of date and scarcely attractive to current sensitivities. Nevertheless, it is having a hard time finding new ones, and so suffers in fear and uncertainty, without models or reference points. He who is a father in the spirit, if he really is such—and the people of God have always shown their ability to recognize him—will not make others equal to himself, but will help them find the way to the Kingdom.

Of course, the wonderful gift of male and female monastic life, which safeguards the gift of guidance in the Spirit and calls for appropriate recognition, has also been given to the West. In this context and wherever grace has inspired these precious means of interior growth, may those in charge foster this gift and use it to good advantage, and may all avail them-

---

31. For example, Anthony's experiences are significant. Cf. Saint Athanasius, *Life of Anthony,* 15: *PG* 26, 865; Saint Pachomius, *Les vies coptes de saint Pakhôme et ses successeurs,* ed. L. Th. Lefort, Louvain 1943, p. 3; and the witness of Evagrius of Pontus, *Practical Treatise,* 100: *SCh* 171, 710.

selves of it. Thus they will experience the great comfort and support of fatherhood in the Spirit on their journey of faith.[32]

Communion and service

14. Precisely in gradual detachment from those worldly things which stand in the way of communion with his Lord, the monk finds the world a place where the beauty of the Creator and the love of the Redeemer are reflected. In his prayers the monk utters an *epiklesis* of the Spirit on the world and is certain that he will be heard, for this is a sharing in Christ's own prayer. Thus he feels rising within himself a deep love for humanity, that love which Eastern prayer so often celebrates as an attribute of God, the friend of men who did not hesitate to offer his Son so that the world might be saved. In this attitude the monk is sometimes enabled to contemplate that world already transfigured by the deifying action of Christ, who died and rose again.

Whatever path the Spirit has in store for him, the monk is always essentially the man of communion. Since antiquity this name has also indicated the monastic style of cenobitic life. Monasticism shows us how there is no true vocation that is not born of the Church and for the Church. This is attested by the experience of so many monks who, within their cells, pray with an extraordinary passion, not only for the human person but for every creature, in a ceaseless cry, that all may be converted to the saving stream of Christ's love. This path of inner liberation in openness to the Other makes the monk a man of charity. In the school of Paul the Apostle, who showed that love is the

---

32. Cf. John Paul II, Homily to Religious, (February 2, 1988), 6: *AAS* 80 (1988), 1111.

fulfilling of the law (cf. *Rom* 13:10), Eastern monastic communion has always been careful to guarantee the superiority of love over every law.

This communion is revealed first and foremost in service to one's brothers in monastic life, but also to the Church community, in forms which vary in time and place, ranging from social assistance to itinerant preaching. The Eastern Churches have lived this endeavor with great generosity, starting with evangelization, the highest service that the Christian can offer his brother, followed by many other forms of spiritual and ministerial service. Indeed it can be said that monasticism in antiquity—and at various times in subsequent ages too—has been the privileged means for the evangelization of peoples.

A person in relationship

15. The monk's life is evidence of the unity that exists in the East between spirituality and theology: the Christian, and the monk in particular, more than seeking abstract truths, knows that his Lord alone is Truth and Life, but also knows that he is the Way, (cf. *Jn* 14:6) to reach both; *knowledge and participation are* thus *a single reality:* from the person to the God who is three Persons through the Incarnation of the Word of God.

The East helps us to express the Christian meaning of the human person with a wealth of elements. It is centered on the Incarnation, from which creation itself draws light. In Christ, true God and true man, the fullness of the human vocation is revealed. In order for man to become God, the Word took on humanity. Man, who constantly experiences the bitter taste of his limitations and sin, does not then abandon himself to recrimination or to anguish, because he knows that within himself the power of divinity is at work. Humanity was assumed by Christ without separation from his divine nature and without confusion,[33] and man is not left alone to attempt, in a thousand often frustrated ways, an impossible ascent to heaven. There is a tabernacle of glory, which is the most holy person of Jesus the Lord, where the divine and the human meet in an embrace that can never be separated. The Word became flesh, like us in everything except sin. He pours divinity into the sick heart of humanity, and imbuing it with the Father's Spirit enables it to become God through grace.

But if this has revealed the Son to us, then it is given us to approach the mystery of the Father, principle of communion in love. The Most Holy Trinity appears to us then as a community of love: to know such a God means to feel the urgent need for him to speak to the world, to communicate himself; and the history of salvation is nothing but the history of God's love for the creature he has loved and chosen, wanting it to be "according to the icon of the Icon"—as the insight of the Eastern Fathers expresses it[34]—that is, molded in the image of the Image, which is the Son, brought to perfect communion by the sanctifier, the Spirit of love. Even when man sins, this God seeks him and loves him, so that the relationship may not be broken off and love may continue to flow. And God loves man in the mystery of the Son, who let himself be put to death on the Cross by a world that did not recognize him, but has been raised up again by the Father as an eternal guarantee that *no*

---

33. Cf. *Symbolum Chalcedonense,* DS 301-302.

34. Cf. Saint Irenaeus, *Against Heresies* V, 16, 2: *SCh* 153/2, 217; IV, 33, 4: *SCh* 100/2, 811; Saint Athanasius, *Against the Gentiles,* 2-3 and 34: *PG* 25, 5-8 and 68-69; *The Incarnation of the Word,* 12-13: *SCh* 18, 228-231.

one can destroy love, for anyone who shares in it is touched by God's glory: it is this man transformed by love whom the disciples contemplated on Tabor, the man whom we are all called to be.

An adoring silence

16. Nevertheless this mystery is continuously veiled, enveloped in silence,[35] lest an idol be created in place of God. Only in a progressive purification of the knowledge of communion, will man and God meet and recognize in an eternal embrace their unending connaturality of love.

Thus is born what is called the *apophatism* of the Christian East: the more man grows in the knowledge of God, the more he perceives him as an inaccessible mystery, whose essence cannot be grasped. This should not be confused with an obscure mysticism in which man loses himself in enigmatic, impersonal realities. On the contrary, the Christians of the East turn to God as Father, Son and Holy Spirit, living persons tenderly present, to whom they utter a solemn and humble, majestic and simple liturgical doxology. But they perceive that one draws close to this presence above all by letting oneself be taught an adoring silence, for *at the culmination of the knowledge and experience of God is his absolute transcendence.* This is reached through the prayerful assimilation of scripture and the liturgy more than by systematic meditation.

In the humble acceptance of the creature's limits before

---

35. Silence *(hesychia)* is an essential component of Eastern monastic spirituality. Cf. *The Life and Sayings of the Desert Fathers: PG* 65, 72-456; Evagrius of Pontus, *The Foundations of Monastic Life*: *PG* 40, 1252-1264.

the infinite transcendence of a God who never ceases to reveal himself as God-Love, the Father of our Lord Jesus Christ in the joy of the Holy Spirit, I see expressed the attitude of prayer and the theological method which the East prefers and continues to offer all believers in Christ.

We must confess that we all have need of this silence, filled with the presence of him who is adored: in theology, so as to exploit fully its own sapiential and spiritual soul; in prayer, so that we may never forget that seeing God means coming down the mountain with a face so radiant that we are obliged to cover it with a veil (cf. *Ex* 34:33), and that our gatherings may make room for God's presence and avoid self-celebration; in preaching, so as not to delude ourselves that it is enough to heap word upon word to attract people to the experience of God; in commitment, so that we will refuse to be locked in a struggle without love and forgiveness. This is what man needs today; he is often unable to be silent for fear of meeting himself, of feeling the emptiness that asks itself about meaning; man who deafens himself with noise. All, believers and nonbelievers alike, need to learn a silence that allows the Other to speak when and how he wishes, and allows us to understand his words.

II

FROM KNOWLEDGE TO ENCOUNTER

17. Thirty years have passed since the bishops of the Catholic Church, meeting in council in the presence of many brothers from other churches and ecclesial communities, listened to the voice of the Spirit as he shed light on deep truths about the nature of the Church, showing that all believers in Christ were far closer than they could imagine, all journeying toward the one Lord, all sustained and supported by his grace. An ever more pressing invitation to unity emerged at that point.

Since then, much ground has been covered in reciprocal knowledge. This has increased our respect and has frequently enabled us to pray to the one Lord together and to pray for one another, on a path of love that is already a pilgrimage of unity.

After the important steps taken by Pope Paul VI, I have wished the path of *mutual knowledge in charity* to be continued. I can testify to the deep love that the fraternal meeting with so many heads and representatives of churches and ecclesial communities has given me in recent years. Together we have shared our concerns and expectations, together we have called for union between our churches and peace for the world. Together we have felt more responsible for the common good, not only as individuals, but in the name of the Christians whose pastors the Lord has made us. Sometimes urgent appeals from other churches, threatened or stricken with violence and abuse, have reached this See of Rome. It has sought to open its heart to them all. As soon as he could, the Bishop of Rome has raised his voice for them, so that people of goodwill might hear the cry of those suffering brothers and sisters of ours.

"Among the sins which require a greater commitment to repentance and conversion should certainly be counted those which have been detrimental to the unity willed by God for his People. In the course of the thousand years now drawing to a close, even more than in the first millennium, ecclesial communion has been painfully wounded, 'a fact for which, often enough, men of both sides were to blame.'[36] Such wounds openly contradict the will of Christ and are a cause of scandal to the world. These sins of the past unfortunately still burden us and remain ever present temptations. It is necessary to make amends for them and earnestly to beseech Christ's forgiveness."[37]

The sin of our separation is very serious: I feel the need to increase our common openness to the Spirit who calls us to conversion, to accept and recognize others with fraternal respect, to make fresh, courageous gestures, able to dispel any temptation to turn back. We feel the need to go beyond the degree of communion we have reached.

18. Every day I have a growing desire to go over the history of the Churches in order to write, at last, a history of our

---

36. Second Vatican Ecumenical Council, Decree on Ecumenism *Unitatis Redintegratio,* 3.

37. John Paul II, Apostolic Letter *Tertio Millennio Adveniente,* (November 10, 1994), 34: *AAS* 87 (1995), 26.

unity and thus return to the time when, after the death and Resurrection of the Lord Jesus, the Gospel spread to the most varied cultures and a most fruitful exchange began which still today is evidenced in the liturgies of the Churches. Despite difficulties and differences, the letters of the Apostles (cf. *2 Cor* 9:11-14) and of the Fathers[38] show very close, fraternal links between the Churches in a full communion of faith, with respect for their specific features and identity. The common experience of martyrdom, and meditation on the acts of the martyrs of every church, sharing in the doctrine of so many holy teachers of the faith, in deep exchange and sharing, strengthen this wonderful feeling of unity.[39] The development of different experiences of ecclesial life did not prevent Christians, through mutual relations, from continuing to feel certain that they were at home in any Church, because praise of the one Father, through Christ in the Holy Spirit, rose from them all, in a marvelous variety of languages and melodies; all were gathered together to celebrate the Eucharist, the heart and model for the community regarding not only spirituality and the moral life, but also the Church's very structure, in the variety of ministries and services under the leadership of the Bishop, successor of the Apostles.[40] *The first councils are an eloquent witness to this enduring unity in diversity.*[41]

---

38. Cf. Saint Clement of Rome, *Letter to the Corinthians: Patres Apostolici,* ed. F.X. Funk, I, 60-144; Saint Ignatius of Antioch, *Letters, l.c.,* 172-252; Saint Polycarp, *Letter to the Philippians, l.c.,* 266-282.

39. Cf. Saint Irenaeus, *Against Heresies* I, 10, 2: *SCh* 264/2, 158-160.

40. Cf. Second Vatican Ecumenical Council, Dogmatic Constitution on the Church *Lumen Gentium,* 26; Constitution on the Sacred Liturgy, *Sacrosanctum Concilium,* 41; Decree on Ecumenism *Unitatis Redintegratio,* 15.

41. Cf. John Paul II, Letter *A Concilio Constantinopolitano* I, (March 25, 1981), 2: *AAS* 73 (1981), 515; Apostolic Letter *Duodecimum Saeculum*, (December 4, 1987), 2 and 4: *AAS* 80 1988, 242.243-244.

Even when certain dogmatic misunderstandings became reinforced—often magnified by the influence of political and cultural factors—leading to sad consequences in relations between the Churches, the effort to call for and to promote the unity of the Church remained alive. When the ecumenical dialogue first began, the Holy Spirit enabled us to be strengthened in our common faith, a perfect continuation of the apostolic kerygma, and for this we thank God with all our heart.[42] Although in the first centuries of the Christian era conflicts were already slowly starting to emerge within the body of the Church, we cannot forget that unity between Rome and Constantinople endured for the whole of the first millennium, despite difficulties. We have increasingly learned that it was not so much an historical episode or a mere question of pre-eminence that tore the fabric of unity, as it was a progressive estrangement, so that the other's diversity was no longer perceived as a common treasure, but as incompatibility. Even when the second millennium experienced a hardening of the polemics and the separation, with mutual ignorance and prejudice increasing all the more, nonetheless constructive meetings between church leaders desirous of intensifying relations and fostering exchanges did not cease, nor did the holy efforts of men and women who, recognizing the setting of one group against the other as a grave sin, and being in love with unity and charity, attempted in many ways to promote the search for communion by prayer, study and reflection, and by open and cordial interaction.[43] All this praiseworthy work was

---

42. Cf. John Paul II, Homily in St. Peter's Basilica, in the presence of Demetrius I, Archbishop of Constantinople and Ecumenical Patriarch (December 6, 1987), 3: *AAS* 80 (1988), 713-714.

43. Cf. for example, Anselm of Havelberg, *Dialogues PL* 188, 1139-1248.

to converge in the reflections of the Second Vatican Council and to be symbolized in the abrogation of the reciprocal excommunications of 1054 by Pope Paul VI and the Ecumenical Patriarch Athenagoras I.[44]

19. The way of charity is experiencing new moments of difficulty following the recent events which have involved Central and Eastern Europe. Christian brothers and sisters who together had suffered persecution are regarding one another with suspicion and fear just when prospects and hopes of greater freedom are appearing: is this not a new, serious risk of sin which we must all make every effort to overcome—if we want the peoples who are seeking the God of love to be able to find him more easily—instead of being scandalized anew by our wounds and conflicts. When, on Good Friday 1994, His Holiness Bartholomew I, Patriarch of Constantinople, offered the Church of Rome his meditations on the Way of the Cross, I recalled this communion in the recent experience of martyrdom: "...We are united in these martyrs from Rome, from the 'Hill of Crosses,' the Solovets Islands and so many other extermination camps. We are united against the background of these martyrs; we cannot fail to be united."[45]

Thus it is urgently necessary to become aware of this most serious responsibility: today we can cooperate in proclaiming the Kingdom or we can become the upholders of new divisions. May the Lord open our hearts, convert our minds and inspire in us concrete, courageous steps, capable if necessary of breaking

---

[44]. Cf. Tomos Agapis, Vatican - Phanar (1958-1970), Rome-Istanbul, 1971, pp. 278-295.

[45]. Address after the Way of the Cross on Good Friday (April 1, 1994): *AAS* 87 (1995), 87.

through clichés, easy resignation or stalemate. If those who want to be first are called to become the servants of all, then the primacy of love will be seen to grow from the courage of this charity. I pray the Lord to inspire, first of all in myself, and in the bishops of the Catholic Church, concrete actions as a witness to this inner certitude. The deepest nature of the Church demands it. Every time we celebrate the Eucharist, the sacrament of communion, we find in the Body and Blood we share the sacrament and the call to our unity.[46] How can we be fully credible if we stand divided before the Eucharist, if we cannot live our sharing in the same Lord whom we are called to proclaim to the world? In view of our reciprocal exclusion from the Eucharist, we feel our poverty and the need to make every effort so that the day may come when we will partake together of the same bread and the same cup.[47] Then the Eucharist will once again be fully perceived as a prophecy of the Kingdom, and these words from a very ancient eucharistic prayer will resound with full truth: "Just as this broken bread, once scattered on the hills and gathered up, became one, so may your Church be gathered from the ends of the earth into your kingdom."[48]

Experiences of unity

20. Particularly significant anniversaries encourage us to turn our thoughts with affection and reverence to the Eastern Churches. First of all, as has been said, the centenary of the

---

46. Cf. *Roman Missal,* Solemnity of the Body and Blood of Christ, prayer over the gifts; *ibid.,* Eucharistic Prayer III; Saint Basil, *Alexandrian Anaphora,* ed. E. Renaudot, *Liturgiarum Orientalium Collectio,* I, Frankfurt, 1847, p. 68.

47. Cf. Paul VI, Message to the Mechitarists (September 8, 1977): *Insegnamenti* 15 (1977), 812.

48. *Didache*, IX, 4: *Patres Apostolici,* ed. F.X. Funk, I, 22.

Apostolic Letter *Orientalium Dignitas*. Since that time a journey began which has led, among other things, in 1917, to the creation of the Congregation for the Oriental Churches[49] and the foundation of the Pontifical Oriental Institute[50] by Pope Benedict XV. Subsequently, on June 5, 1960, John XXIII founded the Secretariat for Promoting Christian Unity.[51] In recent times, on October 18, 1990, I promulgated the Code of Canons of the Eastern Churches,[52] in order to safeguard and to promote the specific features of the Eastern heritage.

These are signs of an attitude that the Church of Rome has always felt was an integral part of the mandate entrusted by Jesus Christ to the Apostle Peter: *to confirm his brothers in faith and unity* (cf. *Lk* 22:32). Attempts in the past had their limits, deriving from the mentality of the times and the very understanding of the truths about the Church. But here I would like to reassert that this commitment is rooted in the conviction that Peter (cf. *Mt* 19:17-19) intends to place himself at the service of a Church united in charity. "Peter's task is to search constantly for ways that will help preserve unity. Therefore he must not create obstacles but must open up paths. Nor is this in any way at odds with the duty entrusted to him by Christ: 'strengthen your brothers in the faith' (cf. *Lk* 22:32). It is significant that Christ said these words precisely at the moment when Peter was about to deny him. It was as if the Master himself wanted to tell Peter: 'Remember that you are weak, that

---

49. Cf. Motu proprio *Dei Providentis* (May 1, 1917): *AAS* 9 (1917), 529-531.

50. Cf. Motu proprio *Orientis Catholici* (October 15, 1917), *l.c.,* 531-533.

51. Cf. Motu proprio *Superno Dei Nutu,* (June 5, 1960), 9: *AAS* 52 (1960), 435-436.

52. Cf. Apostolic Constitution *Sacri Canones* (October 18, 1990): *AAS* 82 (1990), 1033-1044.

you, too, need endless conversion. *You are able to strengthen others only insofar as you are aware of your own weakness.* I entrust to you as your responsibility the truth, the great truth of God, meant for man's salvation, but this truth cannot be preached or put into practice except by loving.' *Veritatem facere in caritate* (To live the truth in love; cf. *Eph* 4:15); this is what is always necessary."[53] Today we know that unity can be achieved through the love of God only if the Churches want it together, in full respect for the traditions of each and for necessary autonomy. We know that this can take place only on the basis of the love of Churches which feel increasingly called to manifest the one Church of Christ, born from one Baptism and from one Eucharist, and which want to be sisters.[54] As I had occasion to say: "the Church of Christ is one. If divisions exist, that is one thing; they must be overcome, but the Church is one, the Church of Christ between East and West can only be one, one and united."[55]

Of course, in today's outlook it appears that true union is possible only in total respect for the other's dignity without claiming that the whole array of uses and customs in the Latin Church is more complete or better suited to showing the fullness of correct doctrine; and again, that this union must be preceded by an awareness of communion that permeates the whole Church and is not limited to an agreement among leaders. Today we are conscious—and this has frequently been reasserted—that unity will be achieved how and when the Lord

---

53. John Paul II, *Crossing the Threshold of Hope* New York 1994, pp. 154-155.

54. Cf. Second Vatican Ecumenical Council, Decree on Ecumenism *Unitatis Redintegratio,* 14.

55. Cf. Greeting to the Faculty of the Pontifical Oriental Institute (December 12, 1993): *L'Osservatore Romano,* December 13-14, 1993, p. 4.

desires, and that it will require the contribution of love's sensitivity and creativity, perhaps even going beyond the forms already tried in history.[56]

21. The Eastern Churches which entered into full communion with Rome wished to be an expression of this concern, according to the degree of maturity of the ecclesial awareness of the time.[57] In entering into catholic communion, they did not at all intend to deny their fidelity to their own tradition, to which they have borne witness down the centuries with heroism and often by shedding their blood. And if sometimes, in their relations with the Orthodox Churches, misunderstandings and open opposition have arisen, we all know that we must *ceaselessly implore divine mercy* and a new heart capable of reconciliation over and above any wrong suffered or inflicted.

It has been stressed several times that the full union of the Catholic Eastern Churches with the Church of Rome which has already been achieved must not imply a diminished awareness of their own authenticity and originality.[58] Wherever this occurred, the Second Vatican Council has urged them to rediscover their full identity, because they have "the right and the duty to govern themselves according to their own special disciplines. For these are guaranteed by ancient tradition, and seem to be better suited to the customs of their faithful and to the good of their souls."[59] These Churches carry a tragic wound, for they

---

56. Cf. Second Vatican Ecumenical Council, Decree on the Catholic Eastern Church *Orientalium Ecclesiarum,* 30.

57. Cf. John Paul II, Message *Magnum Baptismi Donum* (February 14, 1988), 4: *AAS* 80 (1988), 991-992.

58. Cf. Second Vatican Ecumenical Council, Decree on the Catholic Eastern Churches, *Orientalium Ecclesiarum,* 24.

59. *Ibid.,* 5.

are still kept from full communion with the Eastern Orthodox Churches despite sharing in the heritage of their fathers. *A constant, shared conversion is indispensable* for them to advance resolutely and energetically toward mutual understanding. And conversion is also required of the Latin Church, that she may respect and fully appreciate the dignity of Eastern Christians, and accept gratefully the spiritual treasures of which the Eastern Catholic Churches are the bearers, to the benefit of the entire catholic communion;[60] that she may show concretely, far more than in the past, how much she esteems and admires the Christian East and how essential she considers its contribution to the full realization of the Church's universality.

Meeting one another, getting to know one another, working together

22. I have a keen desire that the words which Saint Paul addressed from the East to the faithful of the Church of Rome may resound today on the lips of Christians of the West with regard to their brothers and sisters of the Eastern Churches: "First, I thank my God through Jesus Christ for all of you, because your faith is proclaimed in all the world" *(Rom* 1:8). The Apostle of the Gentiles then immediately and enthusiastically stated his intention: "For I long to see you, that I may impart to you some spiritual gift to strengthen you, that is, that we may be mutually encouraged by each other's faith, both yours and mine" *(Rom* 1:11-12). Here, the dynamic of our

---

60. Cf. Second Vatican Ecumenical Council, Decree on Ecumenism *Unitatis Redintegratio,* 17; John Paul II, Address to the Extraordinary Consistory (June 13, 1994): *L'Osservatore Romano,* June 13-14, 1994, p. 5.

meeting is wonderfully portrayed: knowledge of the treasures of others' faith—which I have just tried to describe—spontaneously produces the incentive for a new and more intimate meeting between brothers and sisters, which will be a true and sincere mutual exchange. It is an incentive which the Spirit constantly inspires in the Church and which becomes more insistent precisely in the moments of greatest difficulty.

23. I am also well aware that at this time certain tensions between the Church of Rome and some of the Eastern Churches are making the path of mutual esteem more difficult with regard to future communion. Several times this See of Rome has made a point of issuing directives favoring the common progress of all the Churches at so important a time for the life of the world, especially in Eastern Europe, where dramatic events of recent history have often prevented the Eastern Churches from properly fulfilling the mandate of evangelization which they nevertheless felt keenly.[61] Situations of greater freedom are offering them fresh opportunities today, although the means available to them are limited because of difficult circumstances in the countries where they are active. I would like forcefully to affirm that the communities of the West are ready to encourage in every way—and many are already working along these lines—*the intensification of this ministry of "diakonia,"* making available to such Churches the experience acquired in the years when charity was more freely

---

61. Cf. John Paul II, *Letter to the Bishops of the European Continent* (May 31, 1991): *AAS* 84 (1992), 163-168; as well as: *General Principles and Practical Norms for Coordinating the Evangelizing Activity and Ecumenical Commitment of the Catholic Church in Russia and in the Other Countries of the C.I.S.,* (published by the Pontifical Commission for Russia on June 1, 1992).

exercised. Woe to us if the abundance of some were to produce the humiliation of others or a sterile and scandalous rivalry. On their part, Western communities will make it their duty above all to share, where possible, service projects with their brothers and sisters in the Eastern Churches, or to assist in bringing to successful conclusion all that the latter are doing to help their people. In any case, in territories where both are present, the Western communities will never show an attitude which could appear disrespectful of the exhausting efforts which the Eastern Churches are making, efforts which are all the more to their credit, given the precariousness of the resources available to them.

To extend gestures of common charity to one another and jointly to those in need will appear as an act with immediate impact. To avoid this or even to witness to the contrary, will make all those who observe us think that every commitment to a *rapprochement* in charity between the Churches is merely an abstract statement, without conviction or concreteness.

I feel that the Lord's call to work in every way to ensure that all believers in Christ will witness together to their own faith is fundamental, especially in the territories where the children of the Catholic Church—Latin and Eastern—and children of the Orthodox Churches live together in large numbers. After their common martyrdom suffered for Christ under the oppression of atheist regimes, the time has come to suffer, if necessary, in order never to fail in the witness of charity among Christians, for even if we gave our body to be burned but had not charity, it would serve no purpose (cf. *1 Cor* 13:3). We must pray intensely that the Lord will soften our minds and hearts, and grant us patience and meekness.

24. I believe that one important way to grow in mutual understanding and unity consists precisely in improving our knowledge of one another. The children of the Catholic Church already know the ways indicated by the Holy See for achieving this: to know the liturgy of the Eastern Churches;[62] to deepen their knowledge of the spiritual traditions of the Fathers and Doctors of the Christian East,[63] to follow the example of the Eastern Churches for the inculturation of the Gospel message; to combat tensions between Latins and Orientals and to encourage dialogue between Catholics and the Orthodox; to train in specialized institutions theologians, liturgists, historians and canonists for the Christian East, who in turn can spread knowledge of the Eastern Churches; to offer appropriate teaching on these subjects in seminaries and theological faculties, especially to future priests.[64] These remain very sound recommendations on which I intend to insist with particular force.

25. In addition to knowledge, I feel *that meeting one another regularly* is very important. In this regard, I hope that monasteries will make a particular effort, precisely because of the unique role played by monastic life within the Churches and because of the many unifying aspects of the monastic experience, and therefore of spiritual awareness, in the East and in the West. Another form of meeting consists in welcoming Orthodox professors and students to the Pontifical Universities and other Catholic academic institutions. We will con-

---

62. Cf. Congregation for Catholic Education, Instruction *In Ecclesiasticum Futurorum*, (June 3, 1979), 48: *Enchiridion Vaticanum* 6, p. 1080.

63. Cf. Congregation for Catholic Education, Instruction *Inspectis Dierum* (November 10, 1989): *AAS* 82 (1990), 607-636.

64. Congregation for Catholic Education, Circular Letter *En égard au développement* (January 6, 1987), 9-14: *L'Osservatore Romano,* April 16, 1987, p. 6.

tinue to do all we can to extend this welcome on a wider scale. May God also bless the founding and development of places designed precisely to offer hospitality to our brothers of the East, including such places in this city of Rome where the living, shared memory of the leaders of the Apostles and of so many martyrs is preserved.

It is important that meetings and exchanges should involve Church communities in the broadest forms and ways. We know for example how positive inter-parish activities such as "twinning" can be for mutual cultural and spiritual enrichment, and also for the exercise of charity.

I judge very positively the initiatives of joint pilgrimages to places where holiness is particularly expressed in remembering men and women who in every age have enriched the Church with the sacrifice of their lives. In this direction it would also be a highly significant act to arrive at a common recognition of the holiness of those Christians who, in recent decades, particularly in the countries of Eastern Europe, have shed their blood for the one faith in Christ.

26. A particular thought goes to the lands of the diaspora where many faithful of the Eastern Churches who have left their countries of origin are living in a mainly Latin environment. These places, where peaceful contact is easier within a pluralist society, could be an ideal environment for improving and intensifying cooperation between the Churches in training future priests and in pastoral and charitable projects, also for the benefit of the Orientals' countries of origin.

I particularly urge the Latin Ordinaries in these countries to study attentively, grasp thoroughly and apply faithfully the principles issued by this Holy See concerning ecumenical cooperation[65] and the pastoral care of the faithful of the Eastern Catholic Churches, especially when they lack their own hierarchy.

I invite the Eastern Catholic Bishops and clergy to collaborate closely with the Latin Ordinaries for an effective apostolate which is not fragmented, especially when their jurisdiction covers immense territories where the absence of cooperation means, in effect, isolation. The Eastern Catholic Bishops will not neglect any means of encouraging an atmosphere of brotherhood, sincere mutual esteem and cooperation with their brothers in the Churches with which we are not yet united in full communion, especially with those who belong to the same ecclesial tradition.

Where in the West there are no Eastern priests to look after the faithful of the Eastern Catholic Churches, Latin Ordinaries and their co-workers should see that those faithful grow in the awareness and knowledge of their own tradition, and they should be invited to cooperate actively in the growth of the Christian community by making their own particular contribution.

27. With regard to monasticism, in consideration of its importance in Eastern Christianity, we would like it to flourish once more in the Eastern Catholic Churches, and that support be given to all those who feel called to work for its revitalization.[66] In fact, in the East an intrinsic link exists between litur-

---

65. Cf. Pontifical Council for Promoting Christian Unity, *Directory for the Application of the Principles and Norms of Ecumenism*, V, *AAS* 85 (1993), 1096-1119.

66. Cf. Message of the Ordinary General Synod of Bishops, VII: "Appeal to Religious of the Eastern Churches" (October 27, 1994): *L'Osservatore Romano*, October 29, 1994, p. 7.

gical prayer, spiritual tradition and the monastic life, For this reason precisely, a well-trained and motivated renewal of monastic life could mean true ecclesial fruitfulness for them as well. Nor should it be thought that this would diminish the effectiveness of the pastoral ministry which in fact will be strengthened by such a vigorous spirituality, and thus will find once more its ideal place. This hope also concerns the territories of the Eastern diaspora, where the presence of Eastern monasteries would give greater stability to the Eastern Churches in those countries, and would make a valuable contribution to the religious life of Western Christians.

Journeying together toward the "Orientale Lumen"

28. In conducting this letter, my thoughts turn to my beloved brothers and sisters the Patriarchs, Bishops, Priests and Deacons, the Monks and Nuns, the men and women of the Eastern Churches.

On the threshold of the third millennium we all hear in our Sees the cry of those oppressed by the burden of grave threats, but who, perhaps even without realizing it, long to know what God in his love intended. These people feel that a ray of light, if it is welcomed, is capable of dispelling the shadows which cover the horizon of the Father's tenderness.

Mary, "Mother of the star that never sets,"[67] "dawn of the mystical day,"[68] "rising of the sun of glory,"[69] shows us the *Orientale Lumen*.

---

67. *Horologion, Akathistos* Hymn to the Most Holy Mother of God, Ikos 5.
68. *Ibid.*
69. *Horologion,* Sunday compline (1st tone) in the Byzantine liturgy.

Every day in the East the sun of hope rises again, the light that restores life to the human race. It is from the East, according to a lovely image, that our Savior will come again (cf. *Mt* 24:27).

For us, the men and women of the East are a symbol of the Lord who comes again. We cannot forget them, not only because we love them as brothers and sisters redeemed by the same Lord, but also because a holy nostalgia for the centuries lived in the full communion of faith and charity urges us and reproaches us for our sins and our mutual misunderstandings: we have deprived the world of a joint witness that could, perhaps, have avoided so many tragedies and even changed the course of history.

We are painfully aware that we cannot yet share in the same Eucharist. Now that the millennium is drawing to a close and our gaze turns to the rising Sun, with gratitude we find these men and women before our eyes and in our heart.

The echo of the Gospel—the words that do not disappoint—continues to resound with force, weakened only by our separation: Christ cries out but man finds it hard to hear his voice because we fail to speak with one accord. We listen together to the cry of those who want to hear God's entire Word. The words of the West need the words of the East, so that God's word may ever more clearly reveal its unfathomable riches. Our words will meet for ever in the heavenly Jerusalem, but we ask and wish that this meeting be anticipated in the holy Church which is still on her way toward the fullness of the Kingdom.

May God shorten the time and distance. May Christ, the *Orientale Lumen,* soon, very soon, grant us to discover that in fact, despite so many centuries of distance, we were very close, because together—perhaps without knowing it—we were walking toward the one Lord, and thus toward one another.

May the people of the third millennium be able to enjoy this discovery, finally achieved by a word that is harmonious and thus fully credible, proclaimed by brothers and sisters who love one another and thank one another for the riches which they exchange. Thus shall we offer ourselves to God with the pure hands of reconciliation, and the people of the world will have one more well-founded reason to believe and to hope.

With these wishes I impart my Blessing to all.

From the Vatican, on May 2, the liturgical memorial of Saint Athanasius, Bishop and Doctor of the Church, in the year 1995, the seventeenth of my Pontificate.

Joannes Paulus PP. II

auline BOOKS & MEDIA

CALIFORNIA
   3908 Sepulveda Blvd., Culver City, CA 90230; 310-397-8676
   5945 Balboa Ave., San Diego, CA 92111; 619-565-9181
   46 Geary Street, San Francisco, CA 94108; 415-781-5180

FLORIDA
   145 S.W. 107th Ave., Miami, FL 33174; 305-559-6715

HAWAII
   1143 Bishop Street, Honolulu, HI 96813; 808-521-2731

ILLINOIS
   172 North Michigan Ave., Chicago, IL 60601; 312-346-4228

LOUISIANA
   4403 Veterans Memorial Blvd., Metairie, LA 70006; 504-887-7631

MASSACHUSETTS
   50 St. Paul's Ave., Jamaica Plain, Boston, MA 02130; 617-522-8911
   Rte. 1, 885 Providence Hwy., Dedham, MA 02026; 781-326-5385

MISSOURI
   9804 Watson Rd., St. Louis, MO 63126; 314-965-3512

NEW JERSEY
   561 U.S. Route 1, Wick Plaza, Edison, NJ 08817; 732-572-1200

NEW YORK
   150 East 52nd Street, New York, NY 10022; 212-754-1110
   78 Fort Place, Staten Island, NY 10301; 718-447-5071

OHIO
   2105 Ontario Street, Cleveland, OH 44115; 216-621-9427

PENNSYLVANIA
   9171-A Roosevelt Blvd., Philadelphia, PA 19114; 215-676-9494

SOUTH CAROLINA
   243 King Street, Charleston, SC 29401; 803-577-0175

TENNESSEE
   4811 Poplar Ave., Memphis, TN 38117; 901-761-2987

TEXAS
   114 Main Plaza, San Antonio, TX 78205; 210-224-8101

VIRGINIA
   1025 King Street, Alexandria, VA 22314; 703-549-3806

CANADA
   3022 Dufferin Street, Toronto, Ontario, Canada M6B 3T5; 416-781-9131
   1155 Yonge Street, Toronto, Ontario, Canada M4T 1W2; 416-934-3440